FUTURISTIC ELECTRIC
Drones

KERRILY SAPET

Mitchell Lane
PUBLISHERS

2001 SW 31st Avenue
Hallandale, FL 33009
www.mitchelllane.com

Copyright © 2020 by Mitchell Lane Publishers. All rights reserved. No part of this book may be reproduced without written permission from the publisher. Printed and bound in the United States of America.

FUTURISTIC ELECTRIC

Library of Congress Cataloging-in-Publication Data
Names: Sapet, Kerrily, 1972- author.
Title: Futuristic electric drones / by Kerrily Sapet.
Description: First edition. | Hallandale, FL : Mitchell Lane Publishers, 2020. | Series: Futuristic electric vehicles | Includes bibliographical references and index.
Identifiers: LCCN 2018028581| ISBN 9781680203523 (library bound) | ISBN 9781680203530 (ebook)
Subjects: LCSH: Drone aircraft—Juvenile literature. | Micro air vehicles—Juvenile literature.
Classification: LCC TL685.35 .S37 2020 | DDC 629.133/39—dc23
LC record available at https://lccn.loc.gov/2018028581

First Edition, 2020.
Author: Kerrily Sapet
Designer: Ed Morgan
Editor: Sharon F. Doorasamy

Series: Futuristic Electric
Title: Drones / by Kerrily Sapet

Hallandale, FL : Mitchell Lane Publishers, [2020]

Library bound ISBN: 9781680203523
eBook ISBN: 9781680203530

PHOTO CREDITS: Design Elements, freepik.com, Cover Photo: Matt Pritchard on Unsplash, p. 5 public domain, p. 6 public domain, p. 9 Diana Macesanu on Unsplash, p. 10 Erik Odiin on Unsplash, p. 11 NOAA public domain, p. 13 LOC public domain, p. 15 Matthew Brodeur on Unsplash, p. 16 markekuliasz, Getty Images, p. 18 Mathias Arlund on Unsplash, p. 19 US Army, p. 21 DARPA, p. 23 Clive Mason/Getty Images, p. 25 freepik.com, p. 26 Ivan Bandura on Unsplash

CONTENTS

Chapter One
FLYING AND SPYING   4

Chapter Two
FROM SEA TO SKY   8

Chapter Three
BIRDS, BATS, AND BUGS   14

Chapter Four
COMING SOON   20

Chapter Five
THE FUTURE OF DRONES   24

WHAT YOU SHOULD KNOW   28
GLOSSARY   29
WORKS CONSULTED   30
FURTHER READING   31
ON THE INTERNET   31
INDEX   32
ABOUT THE AUTHOR   32

Words in **bold** throughout can be found in the Glossary.

Chapter One

FLYING AND SPYING

In 1861, Thaddeus Lowe floated over the White House in a hot-air balloon. President Abraham Lincoln stood on the lawn below. As Lincoln looked up, Lowe sent him a message using the telegraph in the balloon's basket. Lincoln realized hot-air balloons could help win the U.S. Civil War (1861-1865). Lowe could spy from above and send messages to soldiers on the ground. Lowe used his **surveillance** balloons more than 3,000 times. "A hawk hovering above a chicken yard could not have caused more commotion than my balloons," Lowe said.

Aerial surveillance provided valuable information but was dangerous work. Enemy troops tried to shoot balloons down. Some inventors tested unmanned balloons. These balloons carried baskets filled with explosives attached to a timer. The timers were unreliable and the balloons drifted off course. An invention by Nikola Tesla helped control unmanned aerial vehicles or UAVs.

Nikola Tesla was born in Croatia in 1856 during a lightning storm. He would always be fascinated by electricity. Tesla grew up watching his mother invent home appliances. He also built machines—a glider made from an umbrella and a propeller spun by flying June bugs. As an adult, Tesla invented a safer, more powerful, electric motor. "When I get an idea, I start at once building it up in my imagination," he said. "I change the construction, make improvements, and operate the device entirely in my mind."

Nikola Tesla in front of the spiral coil of his high-voltage Tesla coil transformer

CHAPTER ONE

In 1898, Tesla invented the remote control. Using radio waves, his remote control sent signals to a battery-powered boat. The remote control caused "a sensation such as no other invention of mine has ever produced," he said. Some people believed Tesla used mind control powers to move the boat. Tesla predicted his technology would be used to control unmanned vehicles exploring faraway places and fighting wars.

In World War I (1914-1918) and World War II (1939-1945), the military experimented with remote-controlled bombing UAVs. One aircraft, nicknamed "Queen Bee," was used for target practice. Soldiers called unmanned planes "drones," the name for male bees. Soon after, the military developed reusable drones with cameras to take pictures or videos. The drones could launch missiles and conduct surveillance without endangering pilots. Now, drones are doing more than ever before and breaking records for speed and flight time.

British prime minister Winston Churchill (*third from left*) watching preparations being made for the launch of a De Havilland Queen Bee seaplane from its ramp on June 6, 1941. The Queen Bee pilotless target drone was radio-controlled.

Flying and Spying

Today, police send drones to search for missing people, track criminals, and find survivors after disasters. Firefighters use drones to map wildfires. Scientists send drones inside erupting volcanoes. Farmers use drones to check their crops. Moviemakers operate drones to film scenes for movies such as *Black Panther* and *Avengers: Infinity War*. "If you want a moment to look epic, hire a drone," says photographer Parker Gyokeres.

People also fly drones for fun. They use them for racing, snapping pictures, and even catching fish. Drones are delivering pizzas, pollinating orchards, protecting endangered animals, and saving lives. "This is one of the few technologies that could revolutionize the way the world appears," says Mark Blanks, a researcher at Virginia Tech. Many people think electric drones will change lives around the world.

Fun Facts

1 Kongming lanterns, small paper hot-air balloons, were used to signal troops in China more than 2,000 years ago.

2 The Federal Aviation Administration predicts 7 million drones will be flying above American skies by 2020.

Chapter Two

FROM SEA TO SKY

People everywhere, young and old, are flying drones. Drones come in all shapes and sizes. Bug-sized micro drones fit in a pocket and weigh one ounce. Airplane-sized drones weigh thousands of pounds. Some drones look like planes and only move forward. Others resemble helicopters with **rotor blades**. These move in all directions and **hover**. Multicopters have three to eight rotor blades.

Many drones have batteries that power an electric motor. Battery-powered drones fly for 5 to 30 minutes. Gas-powered drones fly for hours or days. Hybrid drones use both electric motors and gas engines. Several companies are also developing solar drones.

Drones can be launched from the ground, dropped from a plane, or tossed into the air. Some drones navigate on their own using **GPS**. Others are guided by pilots using remote controls that look like video game controllers. Pilots control some drones from complex cockpits far from where the drone is flying.

CHAPTER TWO

"During a flight, we are working between multiple computer screens, using drop-down menus, pressing keys, and opening up program menus," says Dennis Rieke, a NASA drone pilot. "It looks just like we are working on computers, but there is a real plane."

Thousands of companies make drones for different uses. Drones can be equipped with cameras, lasers, GPS, and sensors. They conduct research, inspect bridges for safety, help rescue people, deliver packages, and even remove other drones from the sky.

Drones are used to fight wars and spy. They also are used to study parts of the Earth people can't safely visit. Scientists plan to launch electric drones into the waters under the ice in Antarctica. "The environment is just insanely harsh and remote," says Craig Lee of the University of Washington. The drones will explore the canyons beneath the ice, studying the impact of climate change.

From Sea to Sky

The National Oceanic and Atmospheric Administration (NOAA) and Raytheon Missile Systems are using electric drones called Coyotes to track storms.

The Coyotes, launched from NOAA's planes, hover at a storm's edge and collect information about a storm's movement and intensity.

"Drones enable us to get data that is going to protect property and save lives."
—BRIAN ARGROW, DRONE RESEARCHER

Joe Cione of NOAA with a Coyote

CHAPTER TWO

Many companies, such as Amazon and Walmart, are testing drones to deliver packages to customers. In 2018, Boeing released an electric heavy-lifting drone. The car-sized drone can carry 500 pounds.

Other companies are saving lives with drones. Zipline's drones, called Zips, deliver blood, vaccines, and medicines to remote areas in Rwanda. "These are cases where, if bad roads or lack of supply prevents deliveries, people die," says Keller Rinaudo, Zipline's founder. The company plans to start operating in the United States. "We strongly believe that the promise of this technology isn't delivering tennis shoes to your backyard," Rinaudo says.

Ehang is one of dozens of companies testing self-flying passenger drones. Ehang's drone is named 184 because it carries one passenger and has eight rotor blades on four arms. The 184 may be flying the skies by 2019.

Drones are exploring icy waters, zooming into spewing volcanos, and delivering life-saving medicines. They may someday transport passengers between rooftops in cities. Drones are changing the world, with thousands of models taking to the seas and skies.

Fun Facts

In 1906, George Lawrence rigged a camera to 16 kites to take pictures of San Francisco after a devastating earthquake.

From Sea to Sky

PHOTOGRAPH OF SAN FRANCISCO IN RUINS FROM LAWRENCE CAPTIVE AIRSHIP 2000 FEET ABOVE SAN FRANCISCO BAY OVERLOOKING WATER FRONT. SUNSET OVER GOLDEN GATE.

STRANGE SIGHTS

BLINKING LIGHTS. SPINNING OBJECTS. GLOWING ORANGE DISKS. PEOPLE HAVE SPOTTED UNIDENTIFIED FLYING OBJECTS (UFOS) FOR THOUSANDS OF YEARS. MOST SIGHTINGS ARE JUST PLANES, PLANETS, OR METEORS. RECENTLY, UFO SIGHTINGS HIT AN ALL-TIME HIGH. AS MORE DRONES WITH BRIGHT LIGHTS WHIZ THROUGH THE SKIES, MORE PEOPLE THINK THEY ARE SEEING ALIEN SPACESHIPS.

Chapter Three

BIRDS, BATS, AND BUGS

Lift, thrust, drag, and weight. Each **force** affects how a drone flies. Lift holds the drone up in the air. Thrust moves the drone forward. Drag, caused by friction as the drone moves through the air, pushes against the drone. Weight, caused by gravity, pulls down on the drone. The forces work against each other. Heavier drones need more lift to rise into the air. The more a drone drags through the air, the more thrust it takes to move.

Engineers think about the forces when designing drones. The wings or rotor blades create most of the lift. The motor creates the thrust. Drones with more rotor blades produce more lift and fly higher. Drones with more powerful motors go faster and farther. Boeing's heavy-lifting drone has eight spinning blades, each six feet long, to create enough lift to carry 500 pounds. Engineers also work to design **aerodynamic** drones. When air flows smoothly around an object, it has less drag.

The first country to manufacture drones was Israel. The United States built the first armed Predator drone before the terrorist attacks of September 11, 2001, but it was not ready for deployment.

CHAPTER THREE

Many drones use electric motors powered by batteries. The power flows from the batteries to the motors that spin the rotor blades. Drones use rechargeable lithium-ion batteries, like the batteries used in cell phones and computers. Battery chemists are working to develop batteries that weigh less, store more electricity, and charge faster. With better batteries, drones could fly for longer without needing to recharge.

Two lithium-ion polymer rechargeable batteries with balancing and main power plugs

Birds, Bats, and Bugs

What goes up, must come down. After their flights, drones sometimes get stuck in trees, smash into buildings, or crash into people. When they fall, they often break, littering the ground with parts. NASA is creating a **biodegradable** drone that breaks down and doesn't cause pollution. NASA's drone is made of fungus and wasp spit, which wasps use to waterproof their nests. The drone looks like a cardboard drink holder and melts into a pile of mushroom ooze after it crashes. "No one would know if you'd spilled some sugar water or if there'd been an airplane there," says biologist Lynn Rothschild.

To build better drones, scientists are studying flying creatures. "Why not look at animals that have no problem doing this," says David Lentink of Stanford University. Flying insects often hit windows and are fine. Researchers discovered insects' exoskeletons, or outer coverings, are stiff but flexible. Engineers are designing drones with materials that resemble an exoskeleton.

CHAPTER THREE

Scientists are studying how bats fly, turn, and swoop. Engineers are creating a "Bat Bot" with strong carbon fiber bones and joints made of 3D printed plastic, covered with silicon skin. Bat Bots could one day be "aerial service robots at home or in hospitals to help the elderly or disabled by quickly fetching small objects . . . and becoming fun, pet-like companions," says Seth Hutchinson, a robotics engineer. Researchers also are studying vampire bats to build a drone that can fly and walk.

Engineers are using innovative materials to build speedy, strong drones. They are studying nature to design drones that **mimic** animals. Some people predict drones may even become pet-like companions.

Birds, Bats, and Bugs

Fun Facts

1 Most of the lithium used in batteries comes from salt water mines in Chile.

2 Many drones, such as the Raven, Grey Eagle, Black Hornet, and SnowGoose are named after animals.

An RQ-11 Raven Unmanned Aerial Vehicle is launched by Army sergeant Dane Phelps during a joint United States and Iraqi operation in Iraq.

Drones are used in nearly every industry from agriculture to zoology. As more companies look to use drones, thousands of prototypes (new designs) are in progress. Some are still just sketches, others will soon be in use. People around the world are developing prototypes from tiny insect drones to car-sized passenger drones.

While some drones explore the Earth, NASA is testing a drone for their mission to Mars in 2020. The electric drone would fly over Mars' rocky landscape and into lava tubes and deep canyons. NASA is also developing a swarm of Marsbees—bumblebee-size drones with flapping wings like cicadas that could create a 3D map of the planet.

Drones are an important military tool. "Humans make mistakes," says Missy Cummings of Duke University. "We're fragile. We need to eat. We have to sleep. Drones don't need that." The U.S. Air Force is testing swarming drones called Gremlins, named for imaginary creatures that pilots blamed for mechanical problems during World War II (1939-1945). The Gremlins would possibly be powered by hydrogen fuel cells, which combine hydrogen and water to create electricity. Launched from planes, the Gremlins could spy on, attack, or distract enemy troops.

An artist's concept of a C-130 collecting Gremlins after they've accomplished their mission.

CHAPTER FOUR

Many drone prototypes aim to help people. Otherlab, a robotics company, is developing a biodegradable drone called Apsara. A fleet of Apsara drones could be dropped by plane to deliver lightweight emergency supplies. Apsara "looks like a pizza box that's been shaped into a wing," says Star Simpson of Otherlab. The cardboard drone can be built in less than an hour. Apsara is "the world's most functional paper airplane," says Simpson.

Google and Facebook are working on drones to bring Internet access to people in remote areas. Facebook has developed an airplane-sized drone to relay Internet signals. Powered by batteries and solar energy, the drone would provide Internet access for people within 60 miles. Facebook is testing their prototype in Arizona and hopes to have it flying in 2023.

Several companies are designing electric self-flying passenger drones. Most of the prototypes fly a route and sense obstacles, landing and taking off vertically. Kitty Hawk Flyer's prototype resembles a flying motorcycle. Ehang's 184 drone carries one passenger. Ehang has tested the 184 during storms and at night. "This makes you feel like you have travelled into the future, like you're in a sci-fi movie," says Hu Huazhi, Ehang's founder. "But this is real." Ehang's 184 will be out by 2019. Although passenger drones offer a solution to crowded city streets, people worry about safety, noise, and air traffic.

With thousands of prototypes being designed, new drones will soon be flying in a sky near you. Some drones may be controlled by people on the ground. Others may be programmed to fly the people.

Coming Soon

Fun Fact
Drones at Aspire Food Group raise crickets the companies uses to make protein snacks.

SKY-HIGH SHOWS

WITH THE PUSH OF A BUTTON, INTEL'S SHOOTING STAR DRONES RISE INTO THE SKY. IN 2018, THEY PERFORMED LIGHT SHOWS AT THE SUPER BOWL AND THE WINTER OLYMPICS IN PYEONGCHANG, SOUTH KOREA. THE DESIGNS ARE CREATED WITH MORE THAN 1,000 DRONES, EACH WEIGHING ABOUT AS MUCH AS A VOLLEYBALL. "IT CREATES MAGIC IN THE SKIES," SAYS INTEL.

Chapter Five

THE FUTURE OF DRONES

People of all ages in countries around the world fly drones. Some drones fit in the palm of your hand. Other drones fill an airplane hangar. Companies are discovering even more ways to use drones.

Imagine picking up your phone and ordering a pizza. A few minutes later, a delivery drone drops the pizza into your backyard by parachute and sends a text message alerting you that your pizza is ready. Many companies are testing delivery drones and practicing delivering packages to houses and apartments.

Picture climbing to your rooftop and hopping in a passenger drone programmed to take you to the beach. Inside your picnic lunch are apples and almonds pollinated and harvested by drones. This future may not be far away. One out of three farmers uses drones. Passenger drones are being tested in cities around the world, and self-flying drones may soon be buzzing overhead.

"I think it will happen faster than any of us understand. Real prototype vehicles are being built right now."

—DENNIS MUILENBURG, BOEING

CHAPTER FIVE

Drone photos give a different perspective of everyday places.

Although drones help in many ways, they also cause problems. People worry about drones invading privacy or causing injuries when they crash. Sometimes people fly drones dangerously close to planes or airports. There are at least three near-misses between planes and drones every day. Drones may be smaller than airplanes, but they could cause serious damage. "A drone can be like a rock going through the engine," says Javid Bayandor of Virginia Tech.

The Futures of Drones

Most cities, states, and countries have rules about when, where, and how people can use drones. Pilots are not allowed to operate their drones within five miles of an airport or fly higher than 400 feet. They must keep their drone in sight at all times. As more drones fly the skies, lawmakers struggle to keep people safe.

Despite the problems drones may cause, they are here to stay. They reach small spaces and places that are dangerous for people. They entertain people and carry out important jobs. Packed with new technology, the sky is no longer the limit for drones.

Fun Facts

1 In 2018, lifeguards in Australia performed the world's first drone rescue by dropping flotation devices from drones.

2 Drones became illegal in national parks after a drone frightened a herd of big horn sheep, separating lambs from their mothers.

What You Should Know

- In the 1800s, hot-air balloons were used as drones during wars.
- In 1898, Nikola Tesla invented the wireless remote control.
- In the 1900s, wars spurred advances in drone technology.
- Today, millions of people around the world fly drones for work and for fun.
- Many companies are developing self-flying passenger drones.

Glossary

aerial
Happening in the air

aerodynamic
The flow of air around an object

biodegradable
An object that decomposes and doesn't cause pollution

force
The push or pull upon an object

GPS
A system that uses a network of satellites to show a vehicle or person's position (short for "Global Positioning System")

hover
To stay in the air near one place

mimic
To copy

rotor blades
The flat propellers on a helicopter that help it lift into the air and turn

surveillance
A close watch kept over an area or person

Works Consulted

Cherix, Amy. *Eye of the Storm*. Boston: Houghton Mifflin Harcourt, 2017.

Choi, Charles. "Bat Bot Can Pull Off Impressive Aerial Acrobatics." *Live Science*, February 1, 2017.

Dawson, Andy. "Spy Drone Made From Fungus Can Self-Destruct to Avoid Detection." *Mirror* (UK), November 13, 2014.

Doughton, Sandi. "UW's Robotic Fleet Will Probe Under Antarctic Ice Shelves for Clues to Future Sea-Level Rise." *Seattle Times*, December 17, 2017.

Foster, Tom. "Ten Ways Drones Are Changing Your World." *Consumer Reports*, December 14, 2016.

Holmes, Richard. "The Drones of the Civil War." *Slate*, November 21, 2013.

Marsico, Katie. *Inventor, Engineer, and Physicist: Nikola Tesla*. Minneapolis, MN: Lerner Publishing Group, 2017.

Murphy, Mike. "This Might Be the Fastest Delivery Drone in the World." *Quartz*, April 3, 2018.

Soo, Zen. "Flying taxis? Uber has a Competitor in Chinese Drone Maker Ehang." *South China Morning Post*, February 21, 2018.

Further Reading

Abell, Tracy. *All About Drones*. Mankato, MN: North Star Editions, 2017.

Marsico, Katie. *Drones*. New York: Children's Press, 2016.

Rusch, Elizabeth. *Electrical Wizard*. Somerville, MA: Candlewick Press, 2013.

On the Internet

http://howthingsfly.si.edu
A website of the Smithsonian National Air and Space Museum

http://www.alliantenergykids.com/EnergyBasics/AllAboutElectricity
An interactive webpage by Alliant Energy

https://www.nasa.gov/kidsclub/index.html
A kid-friendly website sponsored by NASA

Index

Bat Bot	18	NOAA	11
batteries	9, 16, 19, 22	prototypes	20, 22
Boeing	12, 15, 25	Raytheon Missile Systems	11
Ehang	12, 22	remote control	6, 9, 28
Gremlins	21	Rinaudo, Keller	12
Intel	23	surveillance	4, 5, 6
Lincoln, Abraham	4	Tesla, Nikola	5, 6
NASA	10, 17, 20	Zipline	12

About the Author

KERRILY SAPET graduated from Ohio University. She began writing in 2003 and has authored numerous nonfiction books and magazine articles for kids. She has written about capybaras, queens, racecars, pyramids, and more. Although she doesn't own any drones, she is considering buying one. Sapet currently lives near Chicago, Illinois, with her husband and two sons.